GRANTHAM
AN INDUSTRIAL HERITAGE TRAIL

written by
Peter Stevenson

maps by
Ken Redmor

First Published in Great Britain in 2007 by Society for Lincolnshire History and Archaeology
Text © Peter Stevenson
Design © TUCANN*design&print*

ISBN: 978 0 903582 29 2

Produced by: TUCANN*design&print*, 19 High Street, Heighington Lincoln LN4 1RG
Tel & Fax: 01522 790009
www.tucann.co.uk

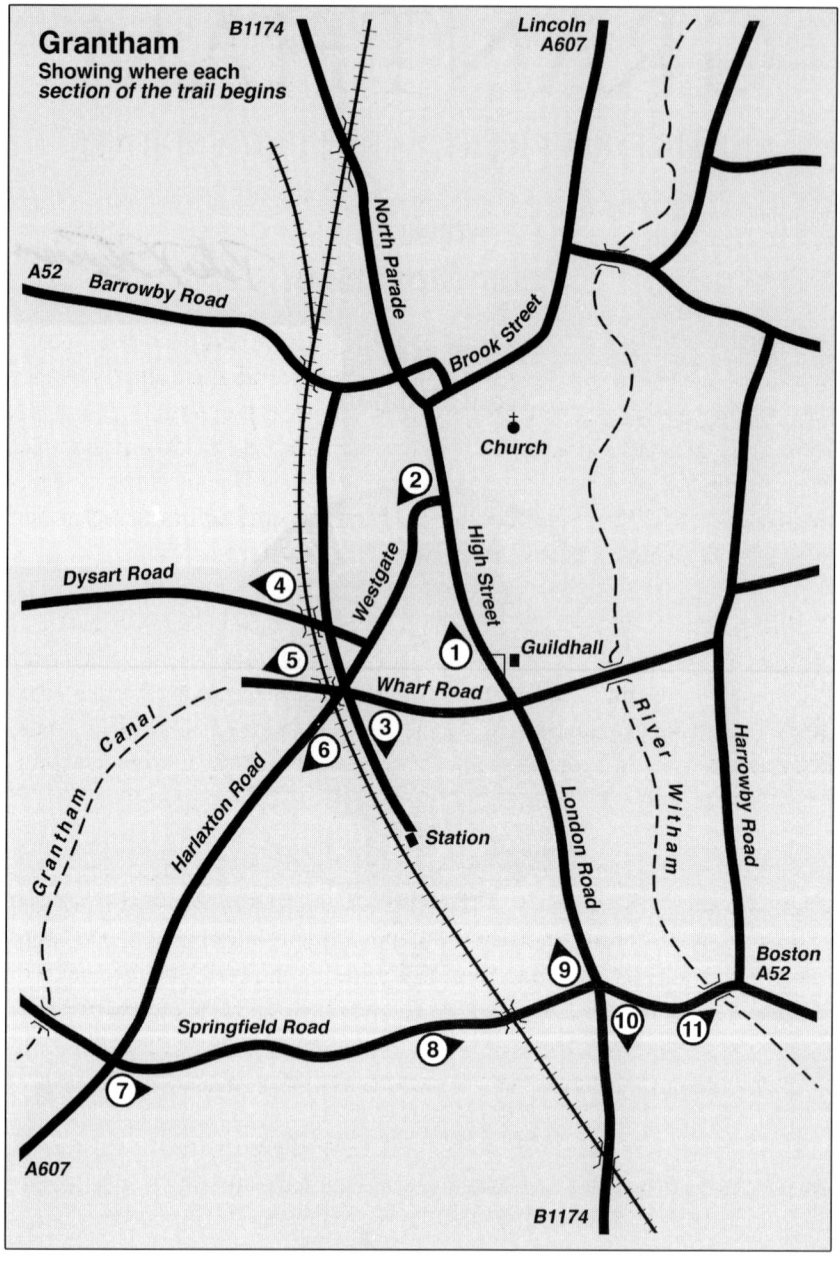

GRANTHAM
AN INDUSTRIAL HERITAGE TRAIL

Sadly, Lincolnshire's second most important industrial town, Grantham has not got a great deal to show today of its industrial past, but what does remain is worth seeking out.

For hundreds of years Grantham had been an important staging post in the long history of the Great North Road, and the rich farmland surrounding it had exported foodstuffs to the great population centres to the south and west. It was natural therefore that, when farming began to be mechanised, Grantham, like many other towns in Lincolnshire, became an important manufacturing centre for agricultural machinery, with products despatched all over Britain and also overseas.

The first spur to Grantham's outward trade came in the 18th century with the construction of the Grantham to Nottingham Canal. This was followed in the mid 19th century with east-west railway links to the newly constructed London to Edinburgh main line. Grantham thus became a focal point for communication and trade and an ideal location for industrial expansion.

Engineering concerns sprang up all over the town, of which the most famous in the 19th and early 20th centuries was that of Richard Hornsby and Sons, who among their many achievements pioneered the design and manufacture of the compression ignition engine. Between the two World Wars new industrial blood came into the town, with internationally renowned companies making road rollers and earth moving machinery, mobile cranes, aircraft cannons and coal mining machinery.

All these manufacturers prospered well until the latter part of the 20th century, when the decline of Britain as a manufacturing nation caused most of them either to move elsewhere or to cease activity altogether. For all that, there is still much to see, or imagine, if you know where to look.

The Angel & Royal Hotel, 15th Century coaching inn, High Street

Harrison shop and works, Watergate

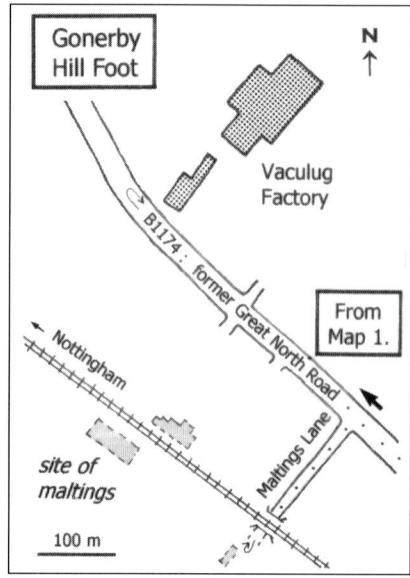

Gonerby Hill Foot

N ↑

Vaculug Factory

B1174 : former Great North Road

From Map 1.

Nottingham

Maltings Lane

site of maltings

100 m

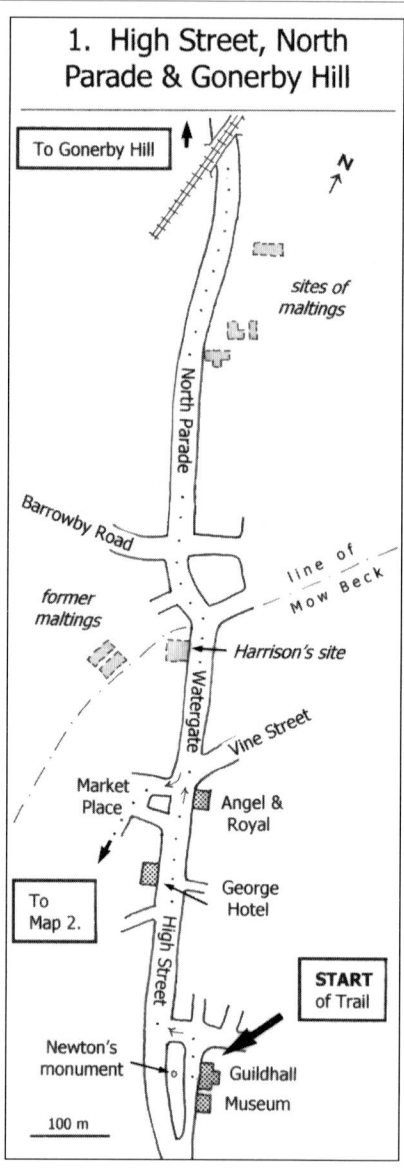

1. High Street, North Parade & Gonerby Hill

To Gonerby Hill

N ↗

sites of maltings

North Parade

Barrowby Road

line of Mow Beck

former maltings

Harrison's site

Watergate

Vine Street

Market Place

Angel & Royal

To Map 2.

George Hotel

High Street

START of Trail

Newton's monument

Guildhall

Museum

100 m

MAP KEY

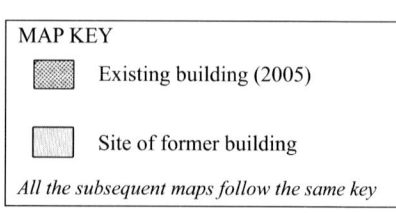

Existing building (2005)

Site of former building

All the subsequent maps follow the same key

THE TRAIL BEGINS on St Peter's Hill in the centre of the town opposite the Guildhall. Walk along High Street in a northerly direction.

Opposite the Victorian Guildhall stands the statue to Grantham's most illustrious son. Born in Woolsthorpe by Colsterworth and educated in Grantham, Isaac Newton went on to formulate the laws upon which all industry is ultimately based.

In those days the Great North Road ran past here and, along this section of the High Street, it would have passed in front of several coaching inns, of which two remain: the George Hotel, Victorian and well-known to Dickens, and the Angel & Royal, historically famous from mediaeval times. The former, opposite the Guildhall, has now been converted into a shopping complex; the latter's imposing façade, further up the street, has an archway leading into a splendid coaching yard complete with stables and other outbuildings, and even the town stocks! Vine Street nearby leads one towards the King's School where Newton studied, in the shade of the great Parish Church.

About half a mile further along, just before the main railway line passes over the former A1, is a side street to the right, Malt Hill, which gives our first clue to Grantham's great past as one of the principal malt producing centres in the midlands. Nineteenth-century trade directories list more than twenty malthouses, of which several once lined Malt Hill.

At the foot of Gonerby Hill stands the Vaculug factory. During World War II this site of a former brickworks was developed into a 'shadow factory', an outstation of BMARC (see page 19), to make ammunition and aircraft cannon components. It subsequently became the headquarter factory of the internationally renowned Vaculug process for the re-treading of large earthmoving tyres. Directly opposite, behind the houses and the far side of the railway embankment, can be found traces of another large malting complex complete with sidings and connections to the main line.

19th C Maltings on Wharf Road, now converted for residential use

Former showroom for Boyall's Coach Works

Boyall's Works bell preserved outside Jewson's store

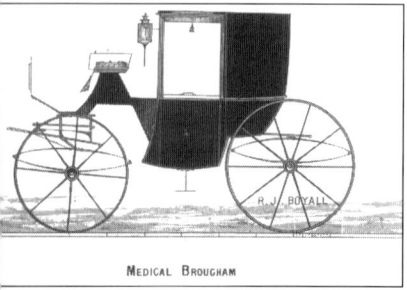

MEDICAL BROUGHAM

Example of carriage from Boyall's catalogue

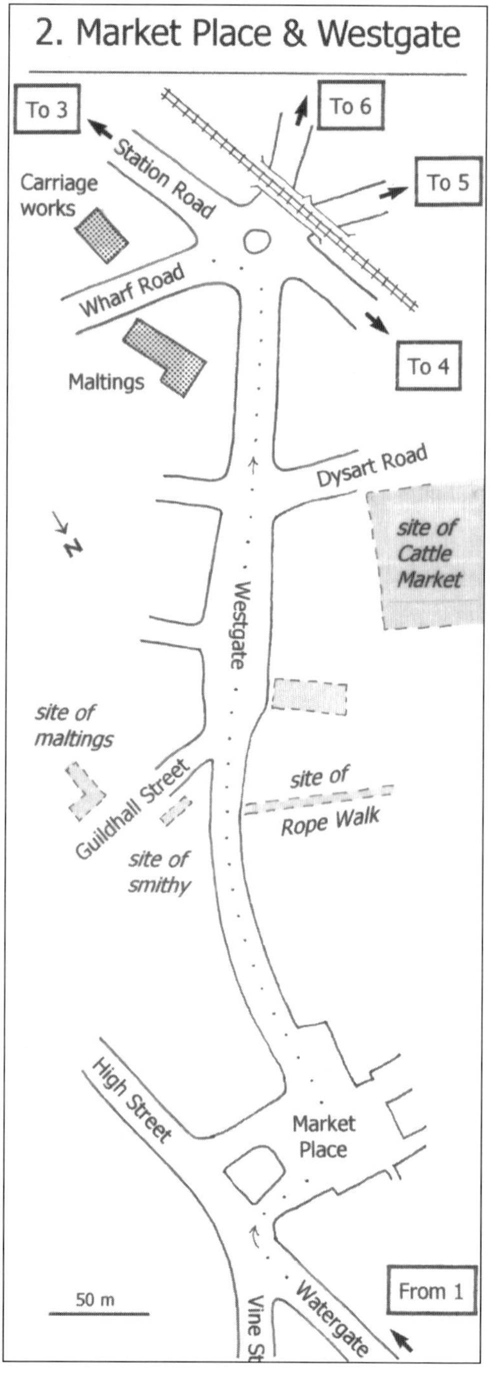

2. Market Place & Westgate

To 3

To 6

Carriage works

Station Road

To 5

Wharf Road

Maltings

To 4

Dysart Road

N

site of Cattle Market

Westgate

site of maltings

Guildhall Street

site of smithy

site of Rope Walk

Boyall's Works bell

High Street

Market Place

50 m

Vine St

Watergate

From 1

Retrace your steps towards the town centre, turning right into the Market Place, then on to the end of Westgate

Watergate, just beyond the traffic lights, was originally called 'Walkergate', for it was here that wool cloth was 'walked' in the now culverted Mow Beck to scour and thicken it. Between here and the Asda supermarket was yet another malthouse, which has now been restored for other uses. Nearby too was the extensive works of Messrs Harrison & Sons, makers of fine cane furniture and a prestigious range of baby carriages.

Old maps and trade directories indicate that occupying the buildings which once lined Westgate, a centre of rural commerce, were many former agricultural 'service industries' such as nail makers, small brass and iron founders, ropemakers, blacksmiths, wheelwrights and the like.

Pause next at the roundabout at the southern end of Westgate. This is truly the focal point of Grantham's early industrial development and within a radius of half a mile or so are the sites and, in some cases, the remains of most of the smaller industrial concerns, some of which gained national and international reputations. This point is overshadowed by the bridges and embankments of the East Coast main line. Roads radiate outwards into what we would today label as 'industrial estates', each road carrying a wealth of industrial history. To one's left is a fine job of urban restoration. The Maltings was a complex of malthouses, now tastefully converted into private accommodation.

Next, find a good excuse to buy something from Jewson's, the builder's merchants, close to the Westgate roundabout. This was the site of Richard Boyall's 'Carriage and Steam Wheel Works'. Between 1860 and 1890 Boyall's produced an extensive range of carriages, artillery wheels and cart components. Their workshops no longer exist but the showroom building, shown in etchings of the time, still remains and has been carefully restored as Jewson's offices and trade centre and is worth looking inside. Just to the right of the shop entrance is the factory bell and across the yard can be seen the traces of the former forge shop with its line of forge chimneys.

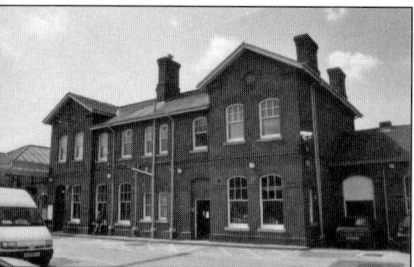

Grantham Station main building

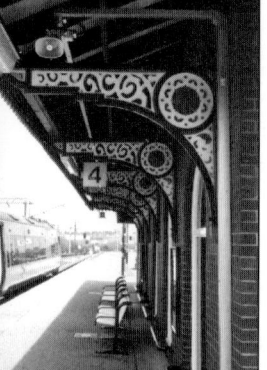

Decorative iron brackets at Grantham Station

JAMES R COULTAS
GRANTHAM

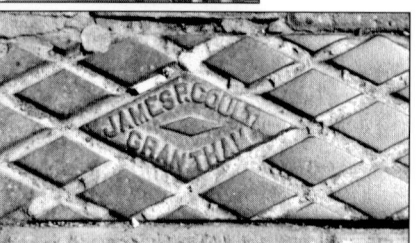

Castings by James Coultas, still to be found in many streets of the town

ROYAL SOCIETY'S PRIZE DRILLS.

Prize-winning seed drill by James Coultas

3. The Railway Station
site of Hornsby's Works
Station Road East
school
Launder Terrace
Grantley House
Map 9
Grantham Station
50 m
N
Site of Perseverence Works (James Coultas)
path
path
Station Road
timber works
Carriage Works
Wharf Road
Maltings
Westgate
From 2
To 4
To 6
To 5

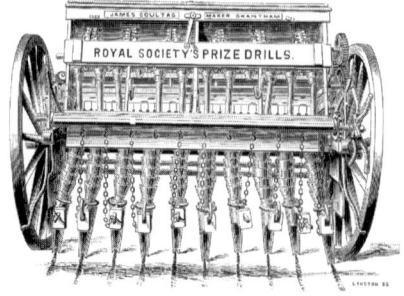

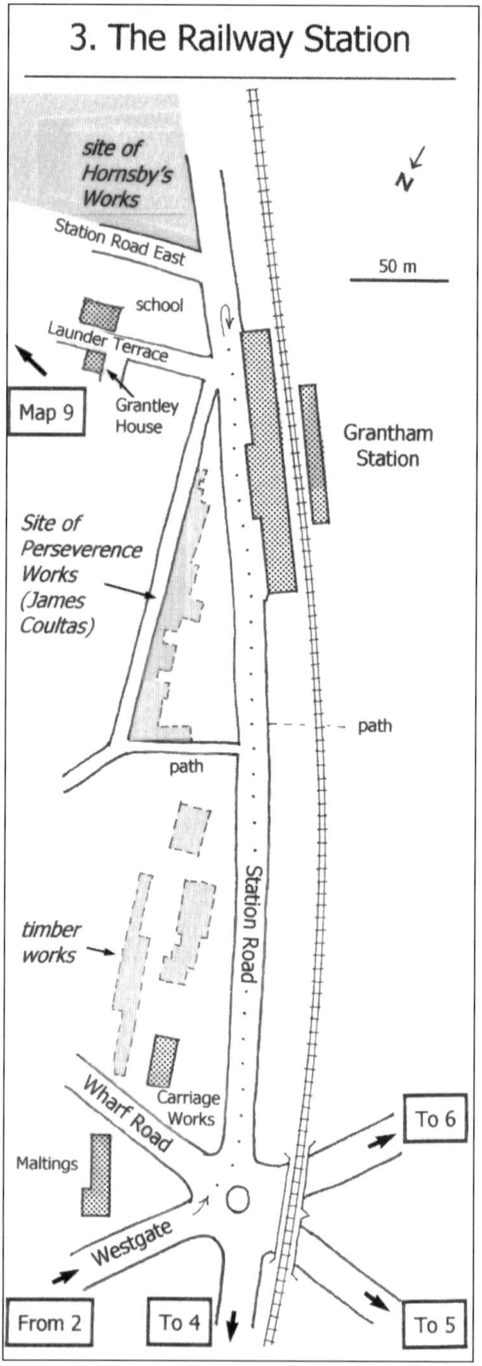

Walk up Station Road

On the left side of Station Road, just above the boundary of Jewson's yard, you will find an area, part of which is given over to station parking. This was the site of James Coultas's 'Perseverence Works', Grantham's second most important agricultural implement manufactory (after Hornsby). For 100 years from the middle of the 19th century the firm produced a wide range of machinery and was outstandingly successful with seed drills and manure distributors, winning a succession of medals at Royal and County Shows.

At the top of the hill is the mainline station. Once the London to Edinburgh line was up and running, Grantham became one of its most important junction stations. Grantham was often the first stop after leaving King's Cross and when the expresses came to a halt, passengers and mail were quickly unloaded. The passengers crossed over to adjacent platforms where connecting trains were waiting to speed them, the mail and other goods, away on branch lines for "all stations to Nottingham, Lincoln, Sleaford and Boston".

Beyond the station a large area, now devoted to further parking, was once completely covered with goods sidings used for handling the tens of thousands of tons of incoming and, above all, outgoing food, raw materials and finished industrial products which passed through Grantham annually. While you are there take a look at the industrial buildings on the left. These are now the upper limit of Hornsby's Spittlegate Works, which we will be visiting later.

Retrace your steps to the roundabout, walk along Sankt Augustin Way a short way and then turn left under the railway bridge into Dysart Road

This is another area of much industrial history. To the left is the long rear wall of one of the workshops of the Grantham Boiler and Crank Co. (see page 15). However, this may soon disappear as the whole area is due for redevelopment as a major shopping centre. A few yards beyond this, on the right, alongside the pavement, can be seen one of the abutments of what was once a railway embankment. Built in the early 1840s, this was the entry point into Grantham of its first railway link to Nottingham. Up to the left was the town's first railway station and its sidings handled most of the freight traffic which had previously been carried by the Grantham to Nottingham Canal.

Railway abutment, near Grantham's first station, Dysart Road

7 NHP portable steam engine by Hempstead & Co, c1880

Grantham Boiler & Crank Company works, Dysart Road (demolished)

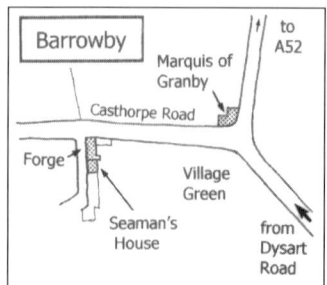

4. Dysart Road

To Barrowby
(2 miles)

Phoenix Iron Works site

→Z

To Canal & Gas Works

former railway

Hempstead Iron Works
(19th century)

Dysart Road

Grantham Boiler & Crank Company
(20th century)

To 5

To 6

Sankt Augustin Way

Westgate

Wharf Road

From 3

50 m

Barrowby

to A52

Marquis of Granby

Casthorpe Road

Forge

Village Green

Seaman's House

from Dysart Road

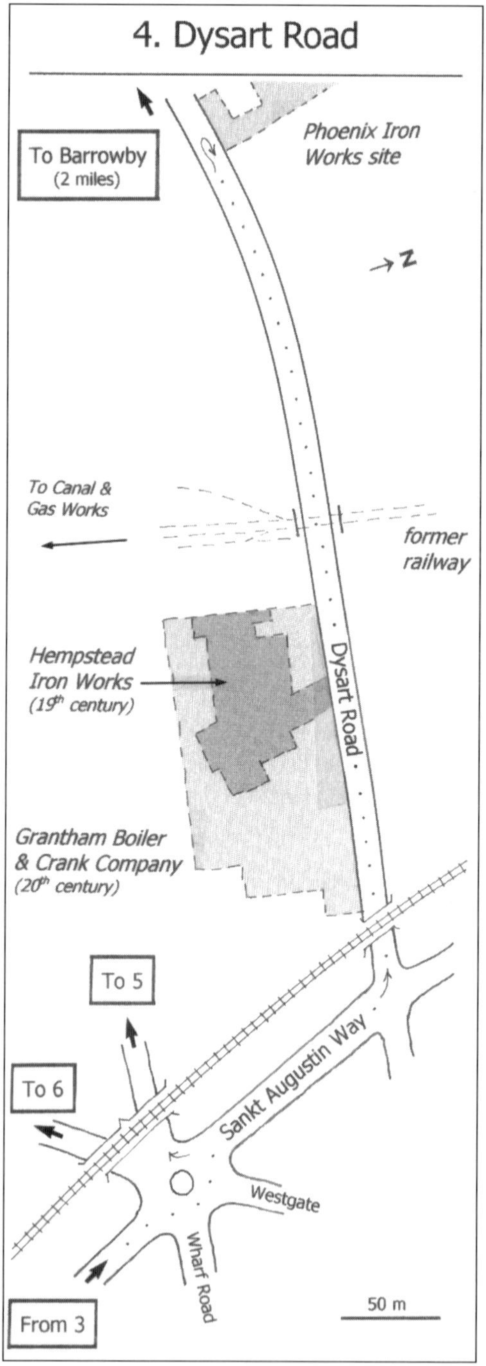

The area higher up Dysart Road is now occupied by a multitude of modern industrial, commercial and transportation concerns, but this has had a long and varied industrial history going back nearly a century and a half. The first developers were two brothers, George and Nathaniel Hempstead, who started a general engineering concern on the site of the Boiler and Crank Works just mentioned. Perhaps unwisely, they built a new works sometime in the 1870s, which they named Phoenix Works; by the end of the century it had closed and appears to have remained so until after World War I. It had a brief revival in the 1920s when it was occupied by the firm of A C Potter. This company made water-well drilling equipment, pumps and other equipment associated with irrigation and drainage, as well as being contractors for their installation. Unfortunately they did not survive the 1930s slump and the Phoenix Works once again became unoccupied.

Then in 1936, when new companies were being encouraged to come to Grantham, the firm of R H Neal took over the Phoenix site to make their range of mobile cranes. This heralded many years of prosperity and expansion. The original Phoenix workshops were demolished and many new shops erected on adjacent land. In the 1960s manufacturing rights for the crawler crane and excavator range of the U.S. based Unit company led to further expansion. A new office block (now occupied by the Woodland Trust) was built. Neal's were then taken over by the Cole's Cranes Group of Sunderland, following which, after a few more years production, the works were slowly run down and then closed. Most of the Neal's/Cole's shops still exist but are now split up into many separate concerns.

If you have the time, carry on up Dysart Road, past all the housing estates, cross over the A1 Grantham by-pass and turn right into the village of Barrowby (about 2 miles). When you come to the village green, turn left onto Casthorpe Road and stop at the end of Mill Lane on the left and take a look at the house called 'The Forge'.

Way back in the 1820s this was the house and workshop of iron worker Richard Seaman, who was well known locally for his workmanship. He was joined by a young apprentice named Richard Hornsby, who was nearing the end of his 'time'. It was not long before he became Seaman's partner and their forge prospered. They decided that they would do better if they moved nearer to the heart of things and so they sold up and moved their work to a new workshop in the then separate village of Spittlegate on the Great North Road, just to the south of Grantham town centre. Here then is the humble starting point of one of the internationally renowned Victorian industrial 'greats', and later on in this trail we will pick up the Hornsby story when we move down to Spittlegate.

Vertical steam engine by Grantham Crank & Iron Co, c1885

Richard Hornsby's first forge and home, Barrowby

Part of Morley's works, Old Wharf Road

20th C corn mills on the site of 19thC Earlesfield Mills, Old Wharf Road

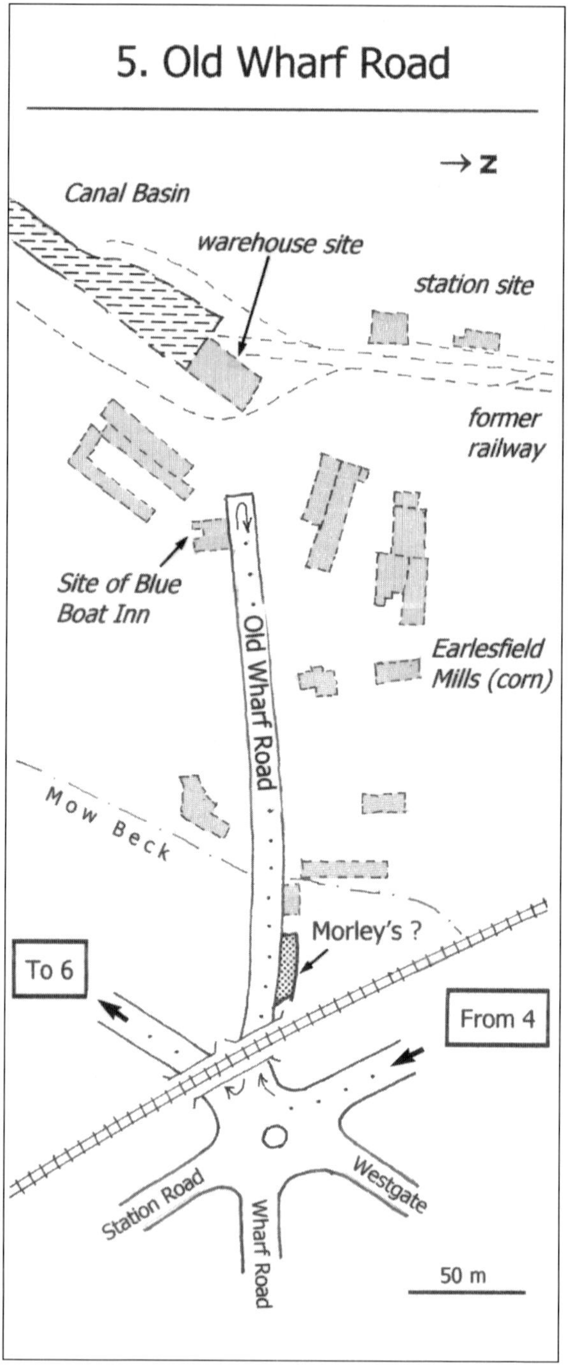

5. Old Wharf Road

→ **Z**

Canal Basin

warehouse site

station site

former railway

Site of Blue Boat Inn

Old Wharf Road

Earlesfield Mills (corn)

Mow Beck

Morley's ?

To 6

From 4

Station Road

Wharf Road

Westgate

50 m

Whether you visit Barrowby or finish at Neal's, go back down Dysart Road and return to the Wharf Road roundabout. Go through the second arch of the mainline bridge and walk up Old Wharf Road.

This was a hive of industry in the late 1700s and the whole of the 1800s. As its name signifies, this led up to the terminal basin of the Nottingham to Grantham Canal. Surrounding this were warehouses, stockyards (for incoming coal, etc.), inns, chandlers, and all the associated services for what was to all intents and purposes a small inland port. With the coming of the railway this area also became the Grantham end of the rail link to Nottingham.

Downhill from this were corn mills and it was here that the Hempstead brothers started their engineering activities. Later, their works were renamed 'Grantham Crank and Iron Co.' and from 1905 'Grantham Boiler and Crank Co.' Under these names, for nearly another century they turned out a mass of engineering products ranging from boilers and crankshaft forgings to bridges. One of their final products before they closed down in the 1970s was the structure of the Cambridge 'Cyclotron' which was involved in much of the earlier work on nuclear physics. Following their closure the works became a steel stockholders and then went into semi-dereliction and, as mentioned earlier, the whole site is due for redevelopment.

Return to the Wharf Road roundabout. This time take the A607 Melton Mowbray Road (Harlaxton Road).

Immediately on the right on what is now a builders' merchant, was once the firm of Yates and Co. They were originally steam ploughing contractors but they soon expanded their workshops to undertake the production of many miscellaneous engineering products. There is also evidence that in this area was another small engineering firm called Morley's, who apparently made small water pumps.

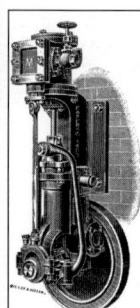

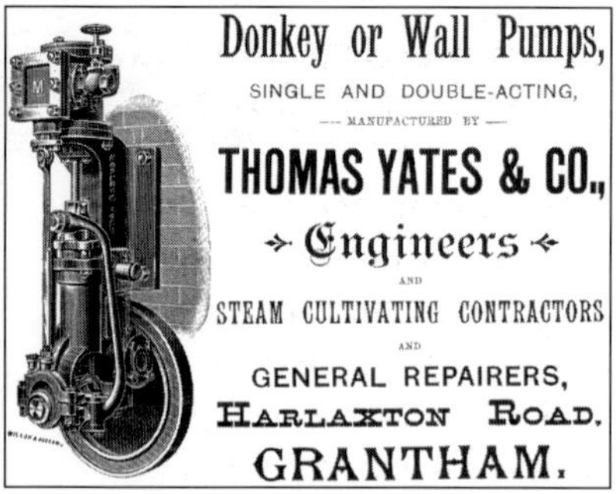

*1896 Advert for Yates & Co,
originally steam ploughing contractors*

*Grantham Canal, from road bridge
on Trent Road (2005)*

*Grantham Gas Company works,
established 1833*

*Advertisement for Shaws'
Leather Works, 1892*

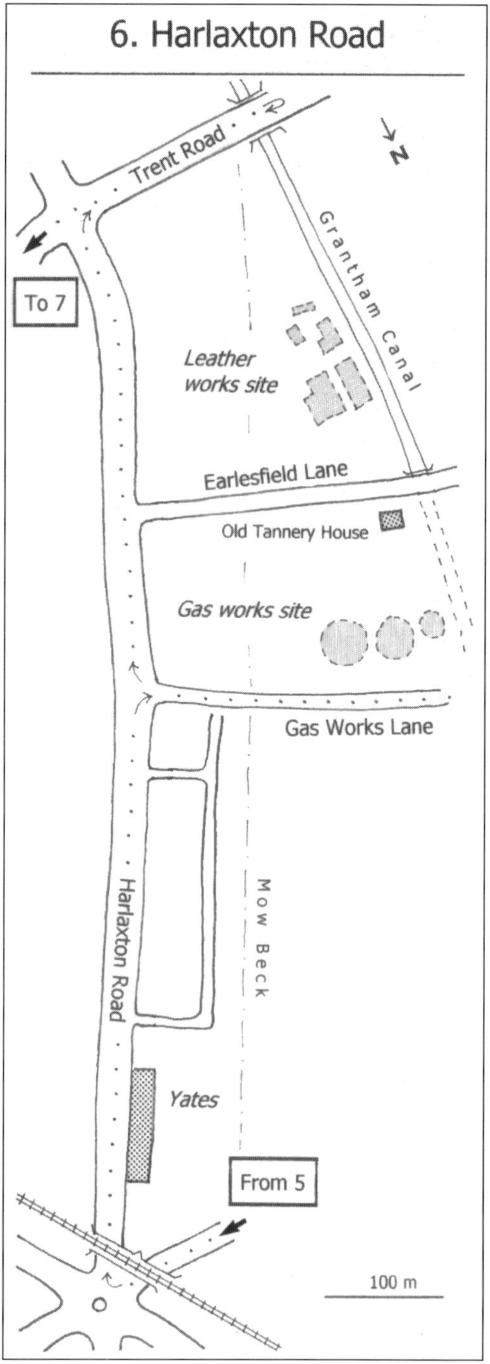

6. Harlaxton Road

Trent Road

To 7

Leather
works site

Grantham Canal

Earlesfield Lane

Old Tannery House

Gas works site

Gas Works Lane

Harlaxton Road

Mow Beck

Yates

From 5

100 m

Make your way along Harlaxton Road until the older terraces of houses end on the right hand side of the road. Walk down the track to the right

This track leads towards the south bank of the canal and at its end is a corral enclosing an imposing array of pipes, valves and other gizmos which is all that remains today of the former Grantham Gas, Light and Coke Company's gas works, which for over a century supplied Grantham's houses, street lighting and industries until natural gas and electrification sealed its doom. In its day, coal came in from the Nottinghamshire coal fields by a railway siding from the Old Wharf Road end of the Nottingham line and canal water was a useful source of process and cooling water.

A little further along Harlaxton Road would have been another entrance leading to a tannery which also made good use of the canal water in its earlier days. This was originally the Earle's Fields' Works of Alexander and John Shaw, 'Fellmongers, Leather Dressers and Parchment Manufacturers and makers of Skivers, Roans and Basils, Aprons, Plasters and Strains, Sod Oil and Splits', whatever they all were! They appear to have operated there for over sixty years between the 1860s and 1920s. In the mid 1930s, another firm encouraged to come to Grantham was the Swedish company Bjorlow, who opened up and modernised the Shaw works and operated there for another thirty years or so. However, this was closed down in the middle of the last century and today no trace remains. The same applies to another small factory also along the south bank of the canal which used to make buttons.

Carry on now to the traffic lights and turn to the right into Trent Road

Pause where Trent Road crosses what now remains as an isolated stretch of the Grantham to Nottingham Canal. Today, this is a haven of peace (if one ignores the traffic noise) but a couple of centuries ago this would have been a scene of an impressive amount of canal traffic. Take one simple statistic: records show that Grantham's exportation of malt products along the canal (before the railways took over) amounted to over fourteen thousand tons annually and it can obviously be assumed that the barges did not come to Grantham empty!

*Granthams last remaining maltings,
Baird's Malt, Springfield Road*

*Part of BMARCO armaments
manufacture complex, Springfield Road
(demolished 2005)*

*Former malthouse, now reused for
light industry, Springfield Road*

*Remaining part of former brick works,
off Springfield Road*

7. Springfield Road (west)

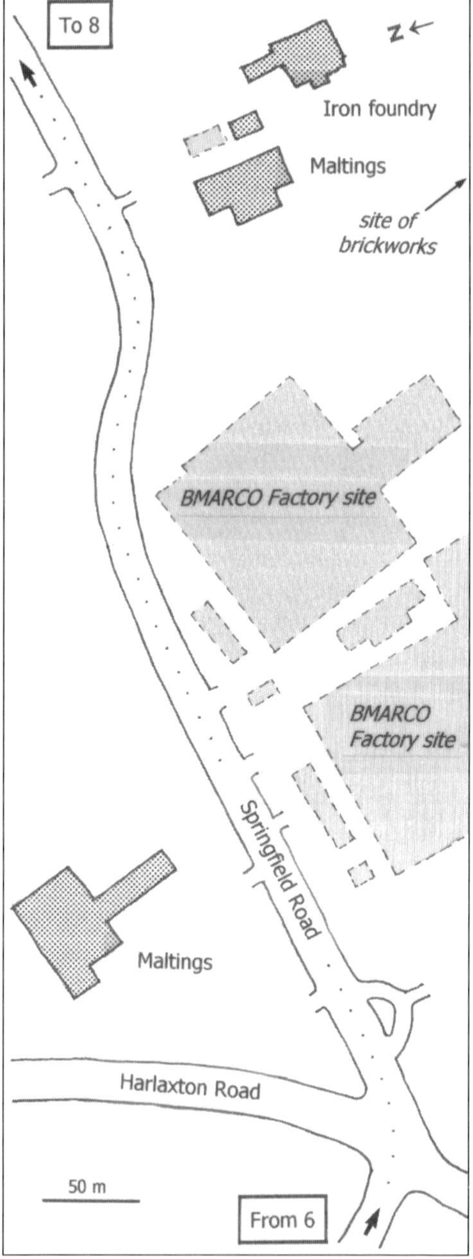

To 8

Iron foundry

Maltings

*site of
brickworks*

BMARCO Factory site

BMARCO
Factory site

Springfield Road

Maltings

Harlaxton Road

50 m

From 6

Retrace your steps from Trent Road and cross over into Springfield Road. Climb up the short hill for about 250 metres and stop opposite the large maltings.

We now take a time leap forward from horse drawn peace and prosperity in the 18th century to war-torn 20th century Grantham. This site on the south side of the road is the former home of the British Manufacturing and Research Company (BMARCO or just 'Marcos' to the Grantham people).

When rearmament began in the 1930s, the need for more powerful fighter aircraft armament than the 0.303in machine gun resulted in the British government setting up a factory for the production of the 20mm Hispanio Suiza aircraft cannon on this site, under the enigmatic title of 'British Manufacturing and Research Company'. This was a completely new type of factory for Grantham: low machine shops full of automatic and semi-automatic machine tools, ammunition filling sheds surrounded by protective blast walls, and even tunnels into the nearby hillside for the testing of finished guns. Grantham soon became accustomed to the heavy roar of these and, as 24 hour working became the norm, Marco's became a non-stop hive of activity. When hostilities began, right from the outbreak this became a prime target for the Luftwaffe. It was bombed several times although even more damage was caused to the town from misdirected bombs.

After the war, an abortive attempt to produce a small 'people's car' and a light tractor (both bearing the name Kendall) merely delayed the closure of Marco's and its conversion to a wide variety of peacetime uses. (We could extend this trail by many miles by routing the tour round the half dozen or so satellite 'Shadow Factories' which were built during the war in the surrounding countryside to disperse production).

Continue along Springfield Road

Next to the BMARC site is an imposing complex of former malthouses which have been largely restored for various uses, including an art and craft centre. The hillside behind these contains a clay band which in earlier times was exploited for brick production. This provided level sites for a number of small industries over the years, and today some of their buildings remain and an iron foundry there still prospers.

19thC Maltings, Spring Gardens

Small remaining part of Hornsby foundry, Spring Gardens

Grantley House, Grantley Street, one time home of Richard Hornsby

Former elementary school, between Launder Terrace and Station Road East

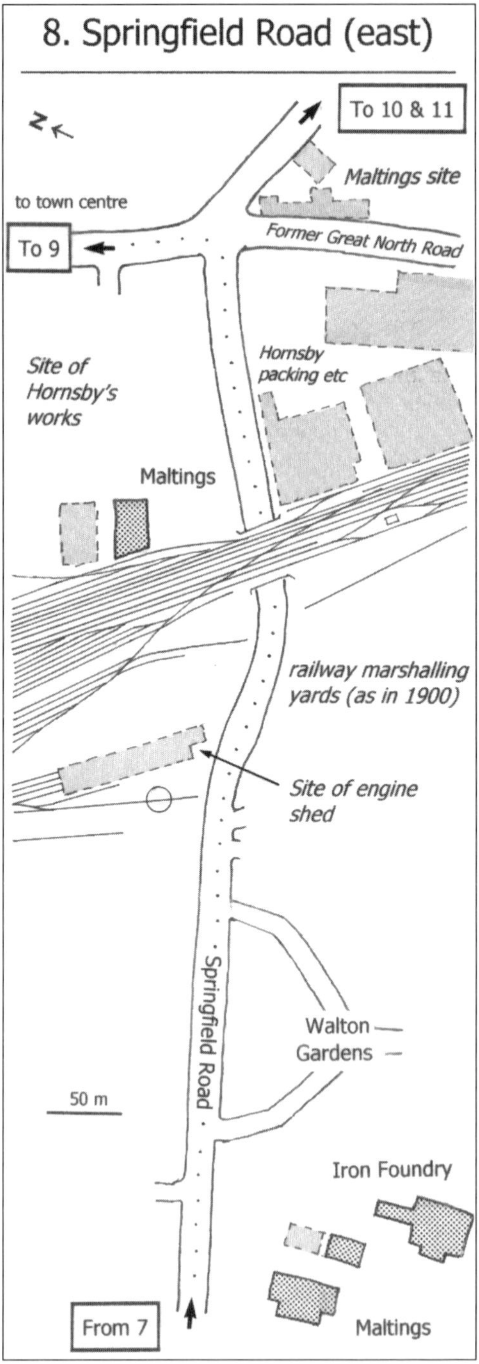

8. Springfield Road (east)

To 10 & 11

Maltings site

to town centre

To 9

Former Great North Road

Site of Hornsby's works

Hornsby packing etc

Maltings

railway marshalling yards (as in 1900)

Site of engine shed

Springfield Road

Walton Gardens

50 m

Iron Foundry

From 7

Maltings

Although not 'industry' as such, the Walton Gardens housing estate on the south side of Springfield Road has a direct link with the town's programme in the mid 1930s to encourage other industry to come to the district. This council house estate was specifically built to house families moving up from Rochester and Peterborough when the new 'Aveling Barford' company was formed and located in the town.

The ground on the opposite (north) side of Springfield Road, now occupied by modern industry and commerce, was formerly the scene of much railway activity. During the steam era Grantham was usually the point where main line express locomotives were changed. 'Train spotting' was carried out by boys of all ages as locomotives were driven into and out of the railway workshops and sheds and also turned round with much 'heave-ho' by the drivers and their firemen on the big turntable.

As you pass under the main line railway bridge over the lower end of Springfield Road you emerge into Spittlegate, the great industrial suburb of Grantham in the 19th and 20th centuries. Today there is little to indicate what you would be seeing if you had been standing at this busy crossroads, say, just before the Second World War. Traffic is bad enough today but then, before the construction of the A1 bypass, north and southbound Great North Road traffic would have been meeting east and westbound traffic from the Boston and Midlands directions.

At the cross roads at the end of Springfield Road turn left into London Road

Looking north along London Road towards the town centre you would be looking along a canyon of factory buildings forming the heart of the Ruston and Hornsby's works. To the right, on the east side of London Road, was the office building which had been formerly the first home and offices of Richard Hornsby, itself on the site of Seaman and Hornsby's first forge buildings after they had moved down from Barrowby in the 1820s. Beyond this, still on the east side, was a long workshop with many chimneys belching smoke, and, above the noise of the North Road traffic, the thumps and other sounds announced that this was Hornsby's forge shop.

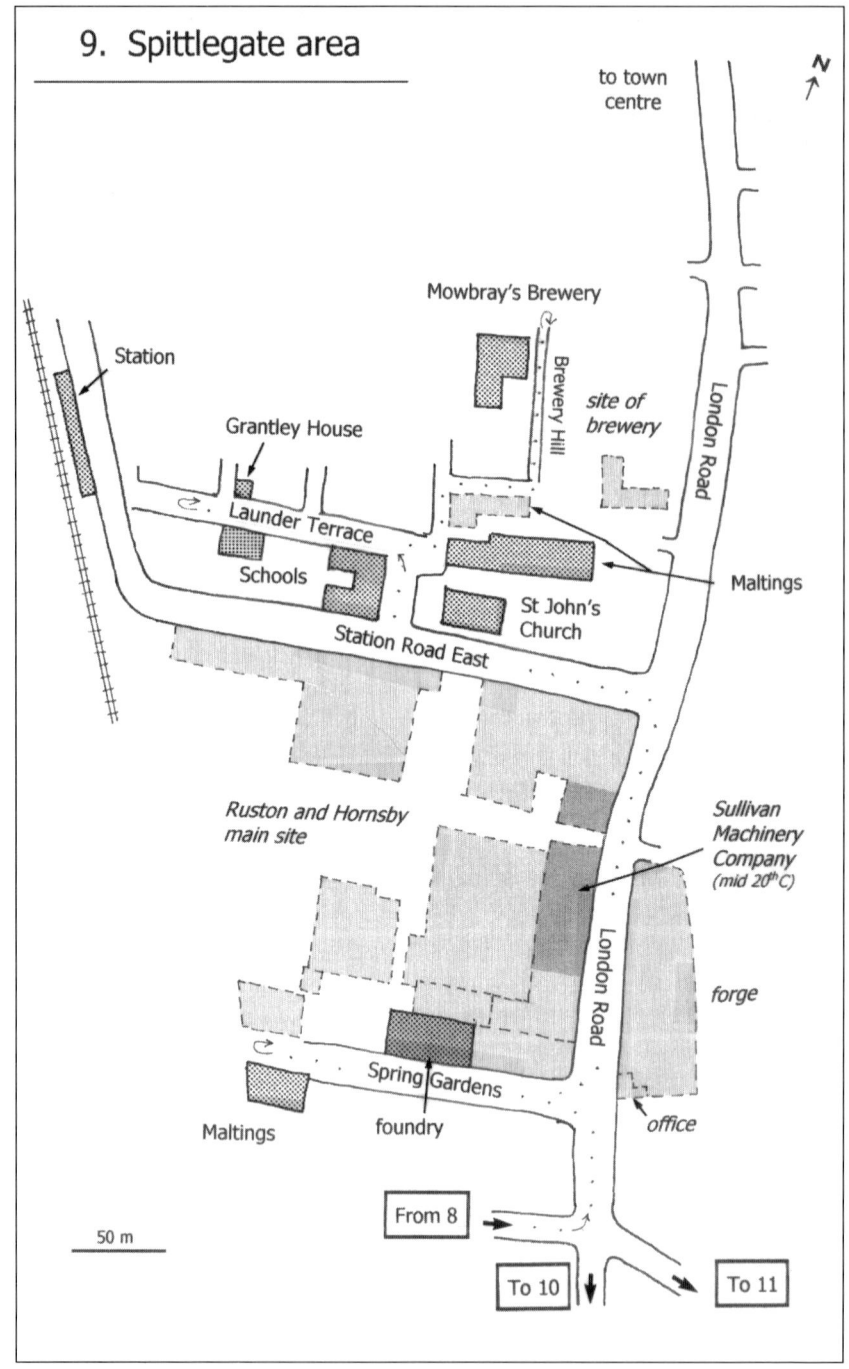

9. Spittlegate area

to town centre

N

Mowbray's Brewery

Brewery Hill

site of brewery

London Road

Station

Grantley House

Launder Terrace

Schools

Maltings

St John's Church

Station Road East

Ruston and Hornsby main site

Sullivan Machinery Company (mid 20th C)

London Road

forge

Spring Gardens

office

Maltings

foundry

50 m

From 8

To 10

To 11

On the west side and opposite to this was an even taller workshop. This was a two-storey building, the upper floor being that of Hornsby's small component 'automatic shop', the lower being leased from Hornsby's by the Sullivan Machinery Co. This was another of the companies persuaded by Grantham Council's drive in the 1930s to bring new industries into the district. For a decade between 1936 and 1946 this American based company made a range of coal cutters and other mining machinery which pioneered the mechanisation of Britain's coal mining and boosted the wartime demand for this vital part of the war effort.

All these buildings have since disappeared to make way for commercial undertakings of many sorts. Those on the east side were demolished during a wartime Luftwaffe attack, the west side when the engineering died out in the latter part of the 20th century. However, the whole area between London Road and the main line railway had been the core of Hornsby's main Spittlegate Works

Take the first road to the left along London Road, called (euphemistically) Spring Gardens

Here you will find some of the original Hornsby workshops still in use for various contemporary industrial and other uses. Also at the top of Spring Gardens was yet another of Grantham's malthouse complexes, one of which still stands in a reasonable state of repair.

Return down to London Road and turn left towards the town centre. Take the next street up to the left - Station Road East.

As you go up Station Road East note the remains of the Hornsby buildings on the left. These represent the northern boundary of the Hornsby works. The gates at the end (if open) lead you into the former station goods yard which we visited earlier on. On the right of the hill as you went up was St John's CE Church and vicarage and above this are the buildings of the former elementary school. All of these buildings were largely financed by Richard Hornsby in late Victorian times.

RUSTON AND HORNSBY WORKS AND PRODUCTS

North-west corner of site, Station Road East (now demolished)

Diesel engine erecting shop, early 20thC

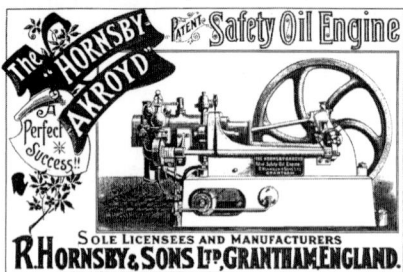

Advert for pioneering Hornsby-Akroyd diesel engine, 1892

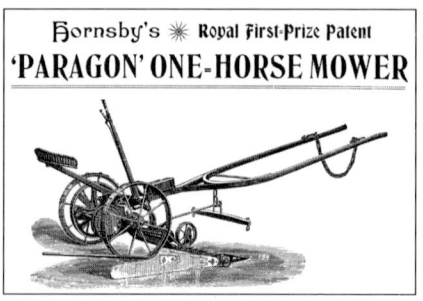

Advert for grass mower, one of many successful agricultural implements

Hornsby's first portable steam engine, 1849

Mining waggons, one of many R & H railway products

Threshing set (traction engine, threshing machine and elevator)

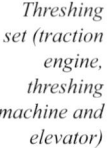

Go past the west front of the church and turn left into Launder Terrace

The second street on the right is Grantley Street which goes northwards down to Wharf Road. On the corner is 'Grantley House' - this was Richard Hornsby's second home when the first on London Road was needed to accommodate the growing office requirements.

Return now to the area just north of St John's Church

Take a look at the maltings here, which have been largely restored and put to other uses. Gradually, over the greater part of the 20th century, the malting industry of Grantham was amalgamated into the firm of Lee and Grinling Ltd., whose headquarters were centred on this site. When this company eventually went out of business, malting in Grantham came to an end, and today nothing remains apart from the many old malthouses which have proved ideal for conversion and occupancy by small industrial and commercial undertakings and for private housing.

Just round the corner to the left is the top of Brewery Hill. As its name indicates, this has been the centre of brewing in Grantham for more than two centuries. Various records show that this street was lined with little breweries and malthouses in the 18th and early 19th centuries but gradually these were amalgamated into one large brewery under the brand name of Mowbray's which used to be one of the premier beer ranges in the East Midlands. Sadly the firm became victim to the 'take over' campaign of the 1960s and for a while produced and traded under the Green's label before, as so often happened, the brewery was closed down and many of its buildings demolished. However, quite a few still remain and these can be compared with advertising etchings in the county guides of the 19th century.

Make your way back down to London Road, turn south towards the crossroads and enter South Parade

This is of course the old Great North Road out of Grantham and from here the signposts used to tell us that it was exactly 110 miles to Charing Cross, from which all milestones were measured.

To the left at the corner of Bridge End Road was, until relatively recently, yet another large malthouse and to the right as one climbs up Spittlegate Hill was an area previously covered with even more Ruston and Hornsby workshops, but they too have gone to be replaced by modern commercial buildings.

*Former Maltings, now head office of
Lee & Grinling Ltd*

*Former Mowbray Brewery buildings on
Brewery Hill*

*Aveling Barford site from the south,
mid 20th Century*

Aveling Barford Diesel Engine Roller, 1930s

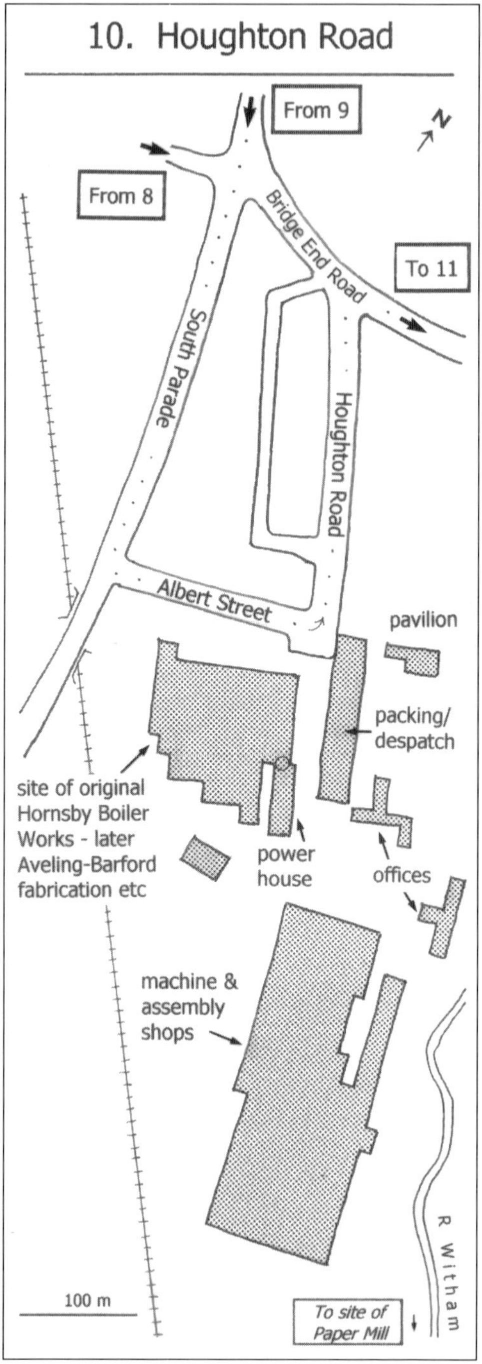

10. Houghton Road

From 9

From 8

Bridge End Road

To 11

South Parade

Houghton Road

Albert Street

pavilion

packing/
despatch

site of original
Hornsby Boiler
Works - later
Aveling-Barford
fabrication etc

power
house

offices

machine &
assembly
shops

R Witham

100 m

To site of
Paper Mill

Just before the main road passes over the main railway to London turn to the left into Albert Street

Here is a typical Victorian factory workers' housing development and at the end of Albert Street, where it joins Houghton (pronounced Hooton) Road, pause a while. To the right one is confronted with the gatehouse to what is still one of the largest factory complexes in Grantham, once the headquarters and principal factory for the production of road rollers (with the legendary brass horse rampant), dump trucks, motor graders and other earthmoving equipment. Aveling Barford Ltd was yet another firm invited to come to Grantham in the mid 1930s. It was formed by the amalgamation of the road roller activities of Aveling & Porter of Rochester, Barford & Perkins of Peterborough and Ruston & Hornsby of Lincoln. The latter company provided its new home from its previous boiler making shop and WWI 'shadow factory' building which was used to make submarine engines.

To learn more about this company, its products and its factory, one could do no better than go to one of the local bookshops and buy the booklet 'The Rise and Fall of Aveling Barford', one of a 'Bygone Grantham' series which give much additional information of the town's past and its industries. Two of these are also devoted to the history of Hornsby's up to 1918 and to Ruston and Hornsby in Grantham following the merger with Ruston's of Lincoln.

Houghton Road is a relatively recent name for the street. For many years this was known as 'Papermill Lane' since, for something like two hundred years, it had led across the fields and down to the banks of the River Witham to what is now called Paper Mill Farm. Richard Hornsby, having in due course bought most of the land in the south of Spittlegate Parish, had acquired the paper mill as well, no doubt finding a useful source of 'bumf' for his growing office activities. In fact for some forty years, between 1840 and 1880, the local gazeteers listed him as being 'Paper Manufacturer' as well as being 'Engineer and Iron Founder'. Nothing now remains of the mill itself apart from some foundations, a weir where the water wheel must have been, and some farm buildings which may have developed from the out-buildings of the paper mill. Some old etchings give an idea of what the mill may have looked like, and the adjacent farmhouse may well have been the mill foreman's house.

St Vincents, former home of Richard Hornsby

11. Bridge End Road & Bridge Street

To **END** of Trail

St Catherine's Road

Dudley Road

N

Maltings
(on Harrow St)

River Witham

100 m

Maltings

Harrowby Road

St Vincent's

From 10

Bridge Street

Spittlegate Mill

Bridge End Road

A52
to Boston

Spittlegate Mill, Bridge End Road, now converted for residential use

Large derelict maltings off Bridge End Road

Rear view of maltings, from Bridge Street

To finish off our odyssey, go down Houghton Road until it joins Bridge End Road, turn right and go on until it crosses the River Witham and pause there awhile

To the right, through overhanging willows, is a thoroughly sylvan scene towards the downstream face of Spittlegate Mill, which is better known to the locals as Swallow's Mill. There have been quite a number of mills on the Witham in the Grantham area, including a slate mill in the northeast outskirts of the town, commemorated today by a cul-de-sac named 'Slate Mill Place', but Swallow's corn mill has always been the most important. Over the years other forms of power have been installed but the waterwheel has been in use within living memory. Today, however, the mill is silent as such and the building has been converted into prestigious apartments.

Whilst we are on the subject of prestigious accommodation, cross over to this bottom end of Harrowby Road. The first turning on the right leads up to St Vincent's, a smallish Victorian mansion which has had a diverse and interesting history. When Richard Hornsby and family had gained fame and fortune, something much grander than Grantley House was needed and some of that fortune went into building St Vincent's. The family used it until the 1920s. Vacant for some years, it was taken over by the R.A.F. and became the headquarters of the legendary No. 5 Bomber Group, which under such leadership as Harris and Cochrane the bombing campaigns of the earlier years of WWII, including the first 'thousand bomber' raids and the Ruhr dambusting, were planned.

In 1943, St Vincent's became the headquarters of the USAAF 9th Troop Carrying Command. Here, too, was the airdrop planning for the Arnhem raid. 'Demobbed', St Vincent's had a variety of uses. For a while it was a Dambusters Museum and then a brief return to industry when it became the headquarters of the Aveling Barford Group, and finally it was converted to private accommodation.

On the opposite side of Harrowby Road can be seen another imposing set of malthouses. Some of these have been converted into industrial and commercial housing. If one goes a few yards up Harrowby Road and turns left into Bridge Street, the rear of this large malting complex can be seen. There had been plans for the whole area to be cleared for new housing but local conservationists won their case and the structure will now be retained and used.

This trail could well have been extended by several more miles, for there are at least the former sites of several more malthouses within the town, several BMARC 'shadow factories', the Grantham Waterworks at Saltersford and so on and so on, but you have seen the essential core. In this respect, should you wish to delve further, may we suggest that you obtain a copy of the recently published 'Guide to the Industrial Heritage of Lincolnshire' obtainable from the Society for Lincolnshire History and Archaeology, Jews' Court, 2-3 Steep Hill, Lincoln LN2 1LS (Tel: 01522 521337).

However, if you have had enough for one day, carry on down Bridge Street, turn right into Dudley Road, then left into St Catherine's Road, and there in front of you will be your starting point at the Guildhall.

Aerial photo of Aveling Barford works from the north